I0181374

The

Scribal Responsibility

Salt, Light, and the

Pursuit of Social Justice

Eual A. Phillips, Jr.

Copyright Notice

The Scribal Responsibility: Salt, Light, and the Pursuit of Social Justice
Copyright © 2023 by Eual Abraham Phillips, Jr.

eual.b.blessed@gmail.com

ISBN (Kindle): 979-8-9892129-2-7

ISBN (Paperback): 979-8-9892129-3-4

KDP ISBN (Hardcover): 9798866820795

ALL RIGHTS RESERVED.   This book contains material protected under International and Federal Copyright Laws and Treaties. Any unauthorized reprint or use of this material is prohibited. No part of this book may be reproduced or transmitted in any form or by any means, electronic or mechanical, including photocopying, recording, or by any information storage and retrieval system without express written permission from the author/publisher, except for the use of brief quotations in a book review.

Typefaces used in this book are Red Hat Text for text and Arvo for display.

Scripture quotations marked (NKJV) are taken from the New King James Version®. Copyright © 1982 by Thomas Nelson. Used by permission. All rights reserved.

Scripture quotations marked (NIV) are taken from the Holy Bible, New International Version®, NIV®. Copyright © 1973, 1978, 1984, 2011 by Biblica, Inc.™ Used by permission of Zondervan. All rights reserved worldwide. www.zondervan.com The "NIV" and "New International Version" are trademarks registered in the United States Patent and Trademark Office by Biblica, Inc.™

Contents

01 – Discover Your Scribal Potential

In the tapestry of life, there exists a profound interconnectedness between the divine and the human, a sacred symphony of spiritual artistry. It is a narrative woven by the ink of faith and the parchment of the heart, and every one of us, regardless of our station in life, possesses the potential to be a scribe in this grand story.

Scribing, or writing, is a privilege and gift from God, bestowed upon us much like the divine endowment of prayer and faith. When adversity besets us, even those who may not direct their petitions to the God who sent Jesus, find solace in the whispered words of a prayer. Faith, a treasure hidden within each heart, is a latent power that not all wield to its full potential. Similarly, the capacity for scribal artistry resides within us all, yet it is not always channeled to benefit humanity.

In the script of our lives, God holds the quill, ready to write upon the tablets of our hearts. A divine calligraphy of love, faithfulness, and eternal truths is etched in the sacred chambers of our souls, as Proverbs wisely reminds us: "Let love and faithfulness never leave you; bind them around your neck, write them on the tablet of your heart." (Proverbs 3:3, NIV)

Yet, in this cosmic narrative, there exists a counterforce. Satan, the deceiver, seeks to usurp the divine calligraphy, inscribing his own dark commands upon the tablets of our hearts. Just as he reimagined God's command for Adam and Eve, he attempted to rewrite the story of Jesus in the wilderness. But Jesus, the embodiment of divine scribal artistry, passed the test.

We, too, possess the capacity to inscribe our intentions, our values, our purpose upon the tablet of our hearts. We are the co-authors of our life's story, for we have the divine prerogative to craft our own narrative. As stewards of our hearts, we are entrusted with the precious treasures God has concealed within us.

As we think, breathe, meditate, and speak, we become the narrators of our lives, wielding the pen of our hearts. The quality of our thoughts and the depths of our beliefs become the crucible in which our moral scribal artistry is forged.

In the covenant of our hearts, God declares, "I will put my law in their minds and write it on their hearts. I will be their God, and they will be my people." (Jeremiah 31:33, NIV) This divine covenant emphasizes that the artistry of the scribe resides within every human heart. It is a birthright, a testament to the divine trust in humanity's capacity to scribe a narrative that aligns with God's purpose.

Thus, as we embark on this journey, let us acknowledge that the heart is the crucible where every person first learns the value of being a scribal artist. Within, God has placed treasures for us to unearth, guard, and preserve. Our thoughts and beliefs form the ink with which we script our lives. Therefore, the extent to which we nurture our hearts, cherish our faith, and express our values will shape the moral compass of our scribal artistry.

The sacred art of the scribe, like prayer and faith, is a gift woven into the very fabric of our existence. This book, "The Scribal Responsibility: Salt, Light, and the Pursuit of Social Justice," will guide you to discover and affirm your inherent scribal artistry.

As we delve into these pages, may you find inspiration, insight, and a deeper connection to your role as a scribal artist, recognizing that your endeavors hold the power to transform society, much like salt and light. Together, we'll explore the pursuit of social justice and the inherent responsibilities that come with wielding the quill, brush, or keyboard.

02 – The Parable of Fading Ink

The Sermon on the Mount, found in the Gospel of Matthew, stands as one of the most iconic teachings of Jesus. In this sermon, Jesus masterfully employed the art of parables to convey profound truths, often in a way that would have left his audience, especially the scribes, astounded. One particular passage, Matthew 5:13-20, serves as an enigmatic masterpiece. Within these verses, Jesus delocalized the power of the scribes by referring to people as the salt of the earth and the light of the world, all while subtly hinting at the enduring nature of his own words and teachings. To fully grasp the brilliance of this hidden parable, we must understand the context and the symbolic significance of salt, light, and the permanence of the message.

In the culture of the time, scribes held a significant place in society. They were the custodians of knowledge and wisdom, wielding immense influence through their command of the written word. Their role included the transcription and preservation of sacred texts, among other duties. Scribes understood the intrinsic qualities of

5

ink, and in particular, the limitations of the ink of their era.

Salt, in Matthew 5:13, holds a symbolic meaning that would not have escaped the scribes. Salt was used as a preservative. It kept food from spoiling and, crucially, prevented decay. By referring to people as the "salt of the earth," Jesus was conveying a profound message. He was saying that the role of preserving God's message and principles was no longer solely in the hands of scribes but was now a responsibility that every believer held. The power to keep the message fresh and uncorrupted had been placed in the hands of ordinary people.

Furthermore, Jesus proclaimed that his followers were the "light of the world." Light has always been a symbol of illumination, clarity, and guidance. By making this declaration, Jesus implied that the knowledge and wisdom he imparted were not confined to the privileged few, but to all who followed him. The light was not hidden under a bushel, but rather set upon a hill for all to see. It was a powerful message that the revelation of God's truth was no longer confined to the scribes' scrolls, but it would be openly accessible and visible through the lives of believers.

Amid these symbolic statements, Jesus dropped an even more subtle clue. He hinted at the endurance of his teachings, stating, "For truly, I say to you, until heaven and earth pass away, not an iota, not a dot, will pass from the Law until all is accomplished" (Matthew 5:18). Here, he was acknowledging the role of scribes and their meticulous transcriptions but also asserting that his teachings and the principles he conveyed would endure beyond mere ink and paper.

This statement would have undoubtedly left the scribes pondering. The ink they used for their writings, known to be composed of ferric sulfate and tannic acid, had a significant limitation. Over time and when exposed to air and light, it would fade. This was a reality that the scribes were aware of, as the very material they worked with had an intrinsic impermanence. However, Jesus was affirming that his teachings would never fade. He was the true source of knowledge and wisdom, and his message would remain vivid and unchanging despite the limitations of earthly ink.

Finally, in Matthew 5:20, Jesus issued a challenge to the scribes and the religious elite of his time. He declared, "For I tell you, unless your righteousness exceeds that of the scribes and Pharisees, you will never enter the kingdom of heaven." Here, Jesus was not undermining the importance of righteousness; instead, he was highlighting that true righteousness was not a matter of adherence to the letter of the law but of embracing the heart of God's message, which he embodied.

In the Sermon on the Mount, Jesus ingeniously delocalized the authority of the scribes, transferring the role of preserving God's message to all believers. He illuminated the truth that the enduring nature of divine wisdom was not bound by the fading ink of human writings but resided in the eternally relevant principles he imparted. The hidden parable within these verses challenged the scribes' conventional authority and beckoned all to be the preservers of righteousness and the bearers of the eternal light of God's wisdom.

03 – Scribing the Divine: Salt, Oil, and the Anointing of the Holy Spirit

Scribal artists, akin to painters, utilize specific compositions, but their canvas is not material—it's the hearts and minds of those seeking to grasp the divine. Let's explore the significance of ink and paint ingredients: salt, oil, and the anointing of the Holy Spirit—within the context of scribes and their sacred mission to preserve and transmit divine messages.

Paint Ingredients: Salt and Oil

In the realm of painting, regardless of the type of paint used, salt and oil are common elements that play crucial roles. Oil acts as a binder, preserving pigments and preventing deterioration. Salt, on the other hand, serves as a preservative, ensuring colors remain vibrant and unfading over time.

Metaphorical Connection to Scribes

In a metaphorical sense, the use of salt and oil in paint relates to the mission of scribes. Just as the right ratio of oils preserves paint quality, scribes are entrusted with preserving and transmitting divine messages. The ink's composition, like paint, must be crafted to withstand external influences and the passage of time, ensuring the message remains vivid and unaltered.

The Role of Salt: Preserving Our Lives and Righteousness

In the spiritual realm, salt symbolizes purity, righteousness, and a preserving influence. Believers are called to be the "salt of the earth" (Matthew 5:13), signifying their role in preserving moral and ethical values. The right balance of salt, akin to the anointing of the Holy Spirit, is essential to maintaining spiritual vitality and moral strength.

The Anointing of the Holy Spirit: Preserving Spiritual Vitality

The anointing of the Holy Spirit is analogous to the use of oils in paint. It is seen as a source of spiritual strength, wisdom, and discernment, empowering believers to stand firm in their faith and values. Just as paint can lose its strength without the right oils, our spiritual lives can lose their vitality and influence without the guidance of the Holy Spirit.

Conclusion: Safeguarding the Divine Message

In essence, the metaphorical connection between the preservation of paint with the right oils, salt, and the anointing of the Holy Spirit underscores the importance of maintaining spiritual vitality, moral strength, and righteousness. Just as paint needs the right oils and salt for preservation, scribes need the presence and guidance of the Holy Spirit to ensure the faithful transmission of divine messages. The ink's composition, like paint, must withstand the tests of time, ultimately fulfilling the sacred mission of scribes in preserving and transmitting the divine message to future generations.

Scribal artists are entrusted with a divine task—similar to painters—working with their unique ink composition to preserve and transmit messages for the benefit of present and future generations. The balance of ingredients in ink, like paint, safeguards the message against the fading influence of external factors and the passage of time. The ink on the canvas of hearts and minds is a sacred endeavor, a work of artistry guided by the divine, ultimately contributing to the fulfillment of God's kingdom characterized by righteousness and justice.

04 – Exploring the Essence of Salt

When we ponder the notion of being the "salt of the earth" and the symbolism of salt and light in Christian teachings, it is often understood that salt enhances flavor and acts as a preservative. While Jesus didn't explicitly refer to salt as a preservative, I will delve into how salt operates as a catalyst for change in its surroundings. Nevertheless, there remain fundamental questions within the body of Christ about what it truly means to be the "salt of the earth," especially for those who see themselves as catalysts for transformation and devout worshipers. Therefore, consider the following:

1: When was the last time you contemplated how salt behaves in different environments and under varying circumstances?
2: Have you ever pondered the intricate workings of taste within the human body?
3: Have you considered the profound implications of salt losing its flavor?
4: Did it ever occur to you that salt can be perceived in places beyond the mouth?

The Hebrew word for "salt" is "melach," which can be dissected into three letters: mem, lamed, and chet. In the Hebrew language, each letter carries its own symbolic significance. Mem signifies water, which can represent the Holy Spirit, water, or chaos, depending on the context. When mem is used as a prefix, it also suggests an origin. Lamed resembles a shepherd's rod, symbolizing authority, control, or a tongue. When lamed precedes another letter, it can imply leadership and movement toward a destination. Finally, chet resembles a fence, signifying separation (Seekins, 1994).

After examining the meanings associated with each of the Hebrew letters in the word "salt," we can present several interpretations that are both valid and valuable for guiding individuals in righteous living. It is essential to remember that salt symbolizes a Christ-centered lifestyle, rather than introducing a "new doctrine" within Christianity. Here are some interpretations to consider:

- Salt is a substance drawn out from the waters by the tongue (or the entire digestive system).

14

- Salt is a substance drawn out from the waters by a rod or staff. Many chemical receptors in the body, including taste receptors, have a rod-like shape.
- Salt is a substance set apart for a specific purpose but requires authoritative guidance to be separated from the waters.
- Salt is a substance set apart for a specific purpose under the leading of the Holy Spirit.
- Salt is authorized for either separation from chaotic waters or navigation through chaotic waters.
- When separated from water, salt creates a fenced structure, known as a crystal lattice in chemistry, which can trap water in certain circumstances.
- Salt has the authority to control the movement of chaotic waters under specific conditions.
- Salt has the authority to facilitate the separation and movement of waters, whether chaotic or Holy Spirit-driven.
- Salt can draw out and contain waters (or spirits) within a fence.

- Salt implies that we are temples capable of housing spirits, and humanity is meant to be a temple for the Holy Spirit.

Salt is a substance with a unique duality, consisting of positive and negative components. Table salt, for instance, is composed of sodium chloride, where sodium represents the positive element and chloride the negative element. Their mutual attraction results in solid salt. However, table salt can easily dissolve in water, allowing water molecules to disrupt this attraction and pull them apart. Therefore, if we are to be like salt, it means we can exist in two states: solid and bound, or dissolved and free.

Let's explore the concept of being bound. When salt is solid or bound, it remains unresponsive to its surroundings. To interact, salt needs to be placed in a specific environment or atmosphere. We have saliva and enzymes to transport our food particles to the appropriate places, enabling us to taste them. Without water, salt would essentially be tasteless. You can strike a large block of salt with a hammer, but it is water that can break the salt apart in a way that makes it ready for consumption.

The essential lesson we can draw from these chemical principles regarding salt is that, as believers in Christ, like salt, our detachment from worldly entanglements allows us to move more freely. We are meant to have a loose attachment to every interaction and live as pilgrims on this earth (Hebrews 11:13; 1 Peter 2:11). Otherwise, if we remain attached to one substance for too long, we risk losing our spiritual flavor.

05 – The Salt of Knowledge: Scribal Artists as Capturers and Distributors of God's Thoughts

In the biblical tradition, salt is not just a seasoning; it is a symbol of both flavor and preservation. In Matthew 5:13, Jesus describes his disciples as the "salt of the earth," emphasizing their role in adding flavor to the world and preserving its moral values. This concept can be extended to the realm of scribal artists, who, like salt, should retain not only flavor but also strength to capture and disseminate the waters of teaching and knowledge to thirsty audiences. Thus, let us explore the multifaceted nature of salt and its profound relevance to the mission of scribal artists.

Salt and Water Capture

Salt and rocks found in the earth possess the remarkable ability to capture water. One notable example of this is in the formation of salt domes, where salt layers trap underground water, creating vast reservoirs. Similarly, porous rocks like limestone absorb water and release it gradually, impacting the local water supply. This natural phenomenon mirrors the role of scribal artists who capture and retain the waters of teaching and knowledge, ultimately shaping the intellectual and spiritual landscape.

God's Thoughts and the Salt of the Earth

Deuteronomy 32:1-2 conveys the idea that God's thoughts are meant to be captured by the salt of the earth: "Let my teaching fall like rain and my words descend like dew, like showers on new grass, like abundant rain on tender plants." Isaiah 55:8-11 reinforces this concept, explaining that God's thoughts are higher than human thoughts and, just as rain and snow water the earth, God's word does not return void but accomplishes its purpose. Scribal artists are entrusted with capturing these divine thoughts and teachings and transmitting them to those in need.

Capturing Righteousness and Justice

Amos 5:24 speaks directly to the importance of righteousness and justice in God's thoughts: "But let justice roll on like a river, righteousness like a never-failing stream!" Scribal artists are called to capture the essence of righteousness and justice and make it part of their message, echoing the divine imperative to promote these ideals in society.

Samaritan Woman at the Well: A Model of Transformation

The story of the Samaritan woman at the well, as described in John 4, offers an exemplary illustration of salt capturing and transforming the waters of Christ. Just as Jesus promised living water to the woman, she received his teachings, absorbed them, and was transformed into a wellspring of knowledge. She then became a fountain pen, so to speak, scribing a short message that captured the hearts of an entire Samaritan community. This narrative underscores the transformative power of God's message when captured by the salt of the earth.

Salt as a Weapon of Captivation

2 Corinthians 10:5 describes the potent use of salt in taking captive every thought and imagination, making them obedient to Christ: "We demolish arguments and every pretension that sets itself up against the knowledge of God, and we take captive every thought to make it obedient to Christ." Scribal artists can wield salt as a weapon to confront and challenge prevailing ideologies and thoughts that deviate from the divine.

Unifying Man's Thoughts with God's

Proverbs 21:1 speaks to the capacity of salt to bring unity between human thoughts and God's thoughts: "The king's heart is a stream of water in the hand of the Lord; he turns it wherever he will." Scribal artists, as agents of God's message, have the potential to redirect the streams of human thought towards the divine, harmonizing human understanding with God's wisdom.

Conclusion

Scribal artists, like the salt of the earth, play a pivotal role in capturing and conveying God's thoughts concerning righteousness and justice. They must act as vessels for divine knowledge and teachings, just as salt captures and releases water. The transformative power of God's message, as seen in the Samaritan woman at the well, serves as a compelling example of what can be achieved through the diligent and faithful work of scribal artists. In the end, it is their duty to be the salt that brings unity between human thought and God's wisdom, preserving the moral values of society and enriching it with the flavor of divine knowledge.

06 – Wavelengths of Light Illuminating Our Paths

Scribal artists hold a unique role in guiding people through their written and artistic expressions, much like God's word illuminates our paths. Psalm 119:105 reminds us, "Your word is a lamp to my feet and a light to my path" (NKJV). To grasp the profound connection between God's word and light, we must understand how light functions and how it parallels the Word of God. Light can be divided into various wavelengths or frequencies, much like the Bible is divided into Old and New Testaments, books, chapters, and verses. Let's explore how each Bible verse carries a unique frequency and wavelength, emphasizing that scribal artists are tasked with conveying these wavelengths of light to illuminate the spiritual paths of their readers.

Wavelengths of God's Word

God's word is, at its core, light. To appreciate this connection, we can draw parallels between light and Scripture. Light can be categorized into various wavelengths or frequencies. Similarly, the Bible is divided into Old and New Testaments, individual books, chapters, and verses. Each verse in the Bible carries a unique frequency and wavelength, signifying that they are individual subdivisions of the divine light.

When we read God's word, we are essentially immersing ourselves in specific wavelengths of light. This intriguing comparison allows us to consider the Bible as a spectrum of spiritual illumination. Just as light is used to detect objects in the physical atmosphere based on the wavelengths absorbed and reflected, we, as readers, can acquire wavelengths of light through our interaction with the Bible. These divine wavelengths enable us to navigate various spiritual atmospheres.

Incomplete Vision and Mastery

However, it is essential to recognize that neglecting certain scriptures is akin to overlooking specific wavelengths of light. If we are not familiar with particular verses or chapters, we remain in the dark concerning the spiritual truths they contain. In essence, without a deep understanding of God's word, we lack the light required to perceive and discern specific aspects of the spiritual realm that are responsive to those missing wavelengths.

The concept that the Old Testament conceals Jesus while the New Testament reveals Him highlights the unique scriptures or wavelengths of light found in each testament. Yet, it is the harmonious interplay between the two that enables us to access the full spectrum of God's divine light. Focusing solely on one aspect while neglecting the other results in an incomplete vision. Scribal artists have a vital role in helping individuals uncover this comprehensive spiritual light.

The Full Counsel of God's Word

When someone speaks of the "full counsel of God's word," they refer to the practice of thoroughly searching the Scriptures without bias, allowing them to address various topics or issues. This comprehensive exploration opens our eyes to the wealth of divine wisdom, guiding us through life's myriad challenges.

However, misinterpreting scriptures can be compared to perceiving one wavelength of light as something entirely different. This misalignment occurs when we fail to compare one wavelength of God's word to another. Our vision becomes distorted, and we may misinterpret the Scriptures. Like any detection system, the more readings we take of a specific wavelength of light, the stronger our understanding of it becomes, whether our interpretation is accurate or inaccurate. This reinforces the importance of thoroughly studying God's word, absorbing its wisdom, and allowing its divine light to illuminate our paths.

Conclusion

Scribal artists, as bearers of God's divine light, play a crucial role in guiding people through the diverse wavelengths of God's word. Just as light consists of various frequencies and wavelengths, the Bible is a rich spectrum of spiritual truth, encompassing both the Old and New

Testaments, each book, chapter, and verse representing a distinct wavelength. Scribal artists should encourage readers to explore the full spectrum of God's light, providing them with an opportunity to draw upon the full counsel of His word.

Misinterpreting Scripture is akin to perceiving one wavelength of light as something entirely different, leading to misaligned spiritual vision. In contrast, a thorough study of God's word, comparing one wavelength to another, results in a more profound understanding and interpretation of divine truths. In essence, scribal artists are tasked with guiding individuals through this intricate tapestry of light, illuminating their spiritual paths and revealing the depths of God's wisdom.

07 – The Metaphor of Light, Justice, and Righteousness

The metaphorical use of light, justice, and righteousness in the Bible carries profound spiritual and moral significance. In particular, the words of Jesus in the Gospel of Matthew, where he calls his followers "the light of the world," echo the prophetic messages from the book of Isaiah that speak of God pouring out His Spirit to establish justice and righteousness. This essay aims to convince scribal artists that Jesus' declaration signifies their active role in establishing His kingdom with justice and righteousness, supported by the anointing of the Holy Spirit. To understand this connection, we'll explore key passages from Isaiah and their alignment with Jesus' message.

The Prophetic Messages of Isaiah:

Isaiah 32:15: Isaiah prophesies about a time when God's Spirit will be poured out, transforming desolation into fertility. The pouring out of the Spirit signifies God's direct intervention to bring life and abundance where there was once barrenness.

This transformation is not just physical but also spiritual, emphasizing the restoration of justice and righteousness.

Isaiah 42:1-4: In this passage, Isaiah speaks of the Servant of the Lord, the chosen one upon whom God will put His Spirit. The outcome of this anointing is the establishment of justice among the nations. The Spirit's presence on the Servant is closely tied to the mission of bringing justice, demonstrating that the Spirit's anointing is intrinsically linked to justice and righteousness.

Isaiah 61:1-3: This passage is especially significant as Jesus Himself applied it to His own ministry. It speaks of the anointing of the Spirit upon the Anointed One, who proclaims good news, binds the brokenhearted, releases captives, and brings transformation from mourning to joy. Notably, it mentions that the result of this work is that those touched by the Spirit will be called "oaks of righteousness" for the display of God's splendor. This reinforces the concept that the Spirit's anointing leads to righteousness and justice being displayed for all to see.

The Forgiveness of Sins and God's Righteousness:

In the context of these prophetic messages from Isaiah and Jesus' declaration, the forgiveness of sins can be seen as an integral part of God's righteousness shining brightly. This concept aligns with the idea that sin, like ink on the tablets of human hearts, can be illuminated and subsequently fade away under the radiance of God's righteousness.

2 Corinthians 3:3 (NIV): "you show that you are a letter from Christ, the result of our ministry, written not with ink but with the Spirit of the living God, not on tablets of stone but on tablets of human hearts."

This verse from 2 Corinthians parallels the idea of God writing on human hearts, not with ink, but with the Spirit of the living God. It implies that the transformative work of the Holy Spirit is at play in inscribing God's truth, justice, and righteousness on the hearts of believers.

The fading of ink, like the fading of sin under the radiance of God's righteousness, can be compared to the process by which traditional iron gall inks fade under exposure to light. Just as light causes the ink to gradually lose its visibility, God's righteousness shining on sin has the power to make sin lose its grip on the human heart. This process of forgiveness and renewal is a testament to the transformative and redemptive power of God's righteousness.

Conclusion

The metaphor of light, justice, and righteousness in the Bible, as seen in the messages of Isaiah and the teachings of Jesus, underscores the profound spiritual and moral role of God's people. When Jesus calls His followers "the light of the world," He is not simply making a poetic statement; He is commissioning them to actively participate in establishing His kingdom with justice and righteousness. The anointing of the Holy Spirit empowers believers to transform a dark world into a place of light and life, where God's justice and righteousness are displayed for all to see. Scribal artists should take this message to heart, as they have a unique role in preserving and spreading the truth, justice, and righteousness found in the Word of God. Just as God's righteousness shines on the ink of sin, causing it to fade, the proclamation of forgiveness and redemption through Christ can bring light and hope to a world in need of God's transformative grace.

08 – Salt, Light, and the Evolution of Scribal Technology

Scribal artists, the bearers of sacred messages, have seen their canvas evolve over time, transitioning from traditional materials like paper and stone tablets to modern photovoltaic canvases that harness the power of light. This transformation mirrors the advancement of communication technologies, emphasizing the unspoken moral responsibility that comes with digital citizenship. In the context of Matthew 5:13-18, let's explore the metaphorical journey of scribal technology, its connection to wireless and Bluetooth communication, and the moral responsibility that accompanies these advancements.

Evolution of the Scribe's Canvas

In the past, scribes and artists relied on materials like paper, parchment, clay tablets, and stone to inscribe their messages. These materials, while valuable, were limited by their physical properties and susceptibility to degradation. Exposure to air and light could cause the salt in the ink, a crucial component, to lose its strength, leading to the disintegration of the medium.

Today, technological advancements have introduced new canvases, such as photovoltaic materials, where salt is sandwiched between layers of plastic and glass, creating solar cells. These cells capture and transform light into energy or images, representing the fusion of art and science. Interestingly, even in our modern digital age, we still utilize the same foundational elements, like salt and oil, albeit in different forms. For instance, the hard drives within electronic devices are composed of various materials, including aluminum alloys, glass, and ceramics, all derived from the essential element of salt.

Metaphorical Connection to Wireless and Bluetooth Technology

The metaphorical connection between evolving scribal canvases and modern communication technologies, specifically wireless and Bluetooth, underscores the unchanging goal of transmitting messages for the purpose of transformation.

Wireless Technology: In the digital age, wireless communication has revolutionized the way we connect. This technology allows messages to travel without physical constraints, much like the evolution of scribal canvases that have enabled the transmission of messages and images without being bound by traditional material limitations. Just as wireless messages travel through the air, we, as scribes, convey messages through the transmission of light, reaching broader audiences than ever before. In a similar vein, scribes have historically aimed to connect with the hearts and minds of people, sharing messages that can inspire transformation through the transmission of the light of God's word.

Digital Citizenship and Moral Responsibility

The evolution of scribal technology has made digital citizenship a reality for nearly every individual in a developed nation. As scribal ministry extends to social media, new moral responsibilities emerge. Just as the Sermon on the Mount can be viewed as a creative teaching that empowered those who had not benefited from spiritual leadership, today's digital citizens inherit the unspoken moral rules for responsible and ethical use of the ancient technology of salt and light.

Goal of Scribal Artistry: Throughout history, whether using traditional or modern mediums, the goal of scribal artistry has been consistent: to craft messages with the enduring strength of the salt of the earth and the radiance of the light of the world. These messages are meant to inscribe themselves on the tablets of human hearts, influencing spiritual and personal transformation.

Conclusion

Advancements in technology demonstrate that scribal artistry remains focused on crafting messages with the enduring strength of the salt of the earth and the radiance of the light of the world. These messages are intended to withstand the tests of time and ultimately find fulfillment, as hinted at in Matthew 5:13-18. The metaphorical journey of scribal technology, from traditional materials to photovoltaic canvases, reflects the progress of communication and artistic expression. In this age of digital citizenship, the unspoken moral responsibilities that accompany our role as salt and light bearers in the digital realm are as significant as ever.

In summary, the evolution of the scribe's canvas from traditional materials to modern photovoltaic technology parallels the advancement of communication and artistic expression. The metaphorical connection to wireless and Bluetooth technology emphasizes the enduring goal of conveying messages of light with the intent of transforming lives and inscribing them on the tablets of human hearts. This responsibility carries deep spiritual significance, as supported by relevant scripture references.

09 – Scribal Legacies of Prophets and Priests

In the Old Testament of the Bible, we encounter a rich tapestry of roles and responsibilities, each intricately woven into the sacred narrative of God's revelation to humanity. Among these roles, the figures of prophets, priests, and scribes stand out as custodians of divine wisdom, tasked with conveying messages, preserving sacred texts, and interpreting God's word. Their collective efforts form the backbone of a timeless mission: to establish a kingdom founded upon principles of righteousness and justice.

Prophets as Scribes

The prophets, chosen by God Himself, were vessels through which divine revelations flowed. They were entrusted with the profound task of recording and delivering God's messages, often in written form, to the people. The written word, penned by these prophetic scribes, served as a testimony for present and future generations.

One remarkable illustration of this role can be found in the book of Jeremiah. The Lord commanded Jeremiah to take a scroll and write down the words He had spoken concerning Israel, Judah, and the nations. This written testimony was to be a lasting witness, embodying the prophetic duty of recording and preserving God's message (Jeremiah 36:2).

The writings of prophets were not merely limited to brief messages. These men of God authored entire books of prophecy. The books of Isaiah, Jeremiah, and Ezekiel, to name a few, exemplify this prophetic role as scribes. Isaiah, in particular, spoke of the birth of a Messiah and the establishment of His kingdom, a testament to the prophetic scribes' commitment to conveying God's grand plan of righteousness and justice (Isaiah 9:6-7).

As custodians of divine revelation, prophets were charged with preserving and transmitting God's word. Their writings continue to be a source of spiritual guidance and profound insight, providing a timeless connection to the principles of righteousness and justice. Moreover, they undertook the task of interpreting and applying God's word within the specific contexts of their time, addressing the pressing needs and challenges of their society.

Priests as Scribes

The priests, serving in a distinct role, operated at the intersection of religion and law. While their primary functions revolved around the administration of religious rites and ceremonies, they also held the mantle of scribes in the realm of preserving and teaching the law. At the heart of their scribal responsibility lay the preservation and transcription of the Mosaic Law, which encompassed the Ten Commandments and a multitude of legal regulations.

The significance of preserving and transcribing the Law is vividly portrayed in the book of Exodus, where Moses, the great lawgiver, is instructed to write down everything that the Lord had spoken. These sacred writings played a pivotal role in shaping the religious and legal landscape of the Israelites (Exodus 24:4).

Moreover, priests held the duty of teaching and explaining the law to the people, ensuring that they understood and faithfully followed God's commandments. In the book of Malachi, the role of the priest as a teacher is emphasized, for the people sought instruction from their mouths, highlighting the profound connection between the role of the priest as scribe and the principles of justice and righteousness (Malachi 2:6-7).

In addition to these responsibilities, priests maintained genealogical records, an essential task for determining tribal and family affiliations, especially in matters related to inheritance and priestly duties. They also recorded rituals and sacrifices performed in the tabernacle or temple, ensuring the religious life of the Israelites was accurately documented. Furthermore, in their role as religious leaders, priests occasionally issued certificates and legal documents, further showcasing the breadth of their scribal responsibilities.

The Collective Legacy: Scribal Responsibilities Unveiled

As we delve into these roles of prophets and priests, we uncover a collective legacy of scribal responsibilities that transcends time. The prophetic scribes, through their recorded messages and books, continue to guide us toward the realization of a kingdom founded on righteousness and justice. The priestly scribes, with their meticulous preservation and teaching of the law, provide a blueprint for understanding and implementing these principles in our lives.

The Bible paints a vivid picture of these roles working in concert to establish a kingdom based on divine wisdom and justice. Prophets, priests, and scribes alike were instrumental in conveying God's plan for a just society, one that would ultimately find its fulfillment in the arrival of the Messiah.

In our contemporary context, we too can embrace these scribal responsibilities. As artists of the written word, creators of content in various forms, we are the torchbearers of this age. Our words, whether written or spoken, have the potential to continue the legacy of scribal artists. Just as prophets and priests recorded and interpreted God's message in their time, we, as modern-day scribes, can carry forward the mission of conveying principles of righteousness and justice, weaving them into the fabric of our society.

Let us draw inspiration from the prophets' unyielding commitment to deliver divine messages and the priests' meticulous preservation and teaching of the law. May we, as scribal artists, recognize our role in the custodianship of wisdom and justice. In doing so, we become active participants in the ongoing narrative of establishing a kingdom founded upon the principles of righteousness and justice, a kingdom that transcends the pages of history and endures through the power of the written word.

10 – Scribal Legacies of the New Testament

In the New Testament, we encounter a tapestry of ideas that echo the timeless theme of God's plan to establish a kingdom rooted in righteousness and justice. However, in this New Covenant, the roles and figures take on a slightly different form, reflecting the transformative ministry of Jesus Christ and His apostles. In this essay, we will explore these concepts through the lens of scribal artists, those who record, interpret, and teach the teachings of Jesus and the principles of God's kingdom.

Jesus Christ as the Fulfillment of God's Plan

In the New Testament, Jesus Christ emerges as the embodiment of God's plan to establish a kingdom based on righteousness and justice. He fulfills the Old Testament prophecies of a righteous and just ruler, the long-awaited Messiah. As a scribal artist of divine wisdom, Jesus often spoke in parables, crafting stories that conveyed the profound principles of righteousness and justice. The Sermon on the Mount, a cornerstone of His teachings (Matthew 5-7), serves as a testament to His role as a masterful scribal artist. In these verses, we find teachings on love, forgiveness, and ethical conduct, exemplifying the essence of a kingdom founded on righteousness and justice.

Apostles as Messengers

Following the resurrection of Jesus, His chosen apostles were entrusted with the sacred task of spreading the message of the Gospel and establishing His kingdom on Earth. They became scribal artists of divine justice, taking the teachings of Jesus and translating them into a practical way of life. Notable apostles like Peter and Paul played pivotal roles in teaching these principles. Their letters, or epistles, provided guidance to early Christian communities, outlining the path toward righteousness and justice. The Book of Acts stands as a record of the apostles' tireless efforts to establish Christian communities, each a brushstroke contributing to the masterpiece of a just and righteous kingdom.

Pauline Epistles

The Apostle Paul, a remarkable scribal artist, left us a legacy of profound letters (epistles) addressed to various Christian communities. His writings elaborated on the importance of righteousness through faith in Christ. Through his teachings, Paul expounded on the profound connection between faith in Jesus and justification. In Romans 14:17, we find his words describing the essence of God's kingdom as being about "righteousness, peace, and joy in the Holy Spirit." This depiction is a testament to Paul's role as a scribal artist, beautifully painting the canvas of God's kingdom.

The Role of the Holy Spirit

The New Testament introduces the Holy Spirit as the guiding force in the lives of believers, empowering them to live righteously and justly. This divine influence, an invisible ink of grace, allows scribal artists of the faith to craft their lives in alignment with God's principles. The Holy Spirit is depicted as a transformative agent, enabling believers to follow the path of righteousness and justice.

Early Christian Communities

The early Christian communities, as depicted in the Acts of the Apostles and the Epistles, serve as living canvases where the principles of righteousness and justice are painted. Acts 2:42-47 beautifully illustrates the ethos of these communities. Believers shared their possessions, met each other's needs, and worshiped together, reflecting a commitment to justice and mutual support. These early Christian communities, like skilled scribal artists, vividly portrayed the ideals of God's kingdom.

Revelation of God's Ultimate Kingdom

The Book of Revelation serves as the masterpiece of apocalyptic artistry, unveiling a vision of God's ultimate kingdom where righteousness and justice reign supreme. This divine artwork, often referred to as the New

Jerusalem, paints a picture of a world where God's righteous rule is established, and justice prevails in all its fullness.

In the New Testament, the role of scribal artists takes center stage. The focus shifts from the Old Testament's system of prophets, priests, teachers, and scribes to the transformative ministry of Jesus and His disciples. They directly taught and demonstrated the principles of righteousness and justice, crafting the narrative of God's kingdom. The New Testament underscores the notion that this kingdom is not just a distant hope but a present reality in the lives of believers, a canvas that scribal artists continue to adorn with strokes of righteousness and justice, shaping the masterpiece of God's eternal kingdom.

11 – Shortcomings of New Testament Scribes

In the New Testament, the Pharisees, Sadducees, and Priests played crucial roles as scribes responsible for preserving and interpreting sacred texts. Their influence on religious and social matters was substantial, yet their positions were not without shortcomings. Recognizing these limitations is pivotal in understanding the multifaceted nature of their scribal artistry and its impact on their religious and societal roles.

The Pharisees

The Pharisees were renowned for their meticulous observance of Jewish law and traditions, and some among them served as scribes. However, their shortcomings included a propensity for legalism, self-righteousness, and hypocrisy. In Matthew 23:23, Jesus rebukes the Pharisees, highlighting their neglect of more critical aspects of the law: "Woe to you, teachers of the law and Pharisees, you hypocrites! You give a tenth of your spices—mint, dill, and cumin. But you have neglected the more important matters of the law—justice, mercy, and faithfulness. You should have practiced the latter without neglecting the former." Jesus also critiqued their outward displays of piety, emphasizing the importance of authentic transformation of the heart (Matthew 23:5-7). Their obsession with the minutiae of the law often led to rigid and inflexible interpretations, devoid of the compassion and mercy central to the teachings of the Scriptures. Their failure to embody the spirit of the law, focusing on external rituals, risked undermining the genuine depth of their scribal artistry. Their fixation on doctrinal purity might have resulted in an overemphasis on rules, potentially obscuring the profound spiritual messages of the texts they were tasked with preserving and interpreting.

The Sadducees

The Sadducees held conservative theological views and were primarily associated with the priestly class. Their main shortcoming lay in their skepticism regarding key doctrinal elements, such as the resurrection of the dead. In Matthew

22:29, Jesus chastises the Sadducees for their disbelief in the resurrection: "You are in error because you do not know the Scriptures or the power of God." This skepticism could have influenced their approach to scriptural interpretation, potentially leading to selective readings or outright dismissal of passages that conflicted with their beliefs. Their role in Temple administration further detached them from broader religious concerns, potentially affecting their understanding of the needs and concerns of ordinary people. Consequently, their scribal artistry might have been influenced by doctrinal bias and a lack of inclusivity.

The Priests

The priests, as the custodians of the Temple, were responsible for offering sacrifices and conducting religious rituals. While they possessed a profound understanding of the Temple's significance, their engagement with the broader body of sacred texts might have been limited. Their primary focus on ritual and sacrificial matters could have hindered their ability to engage in the depth of textual analysis and interpretation expected of scribes. Although the priests were responsible for carrying out temple worship and sacrifices, they were not immune to moral failings. In the parable of the Good Samaritan (Luke 10:25-37), a priest passes by a wounded man without offering assistance, while a despised Samaritan demonstrates compassion and justice. This episode underscores the failure of the priestly class to fulfill their role in caring for the marginalized. Their immersion in the Temple environment could also create a certain distance from the daily lives and struggles of the common people, potentially affecting the relevance and relatability of their scribal work.

In all three cases, the shortcomings of these groups could impact their scribal artistry in various ways. Their narrow interpretations, influenced by rigid legalism (Pharisees), theological skepticism (Sadducees), or a focus on ritual (Priests), might limit the depth and breadth of their engagement with the sacred texts. This could lead to a lack of nuance in their interpretations, and they might prioritize dogma over the spirit and intent of the scriptures.

Furthermore, these groups' societal positions and privileges might lead to a degree of disconnect from the everyday concerns of the people they served. This disconnect could result in a lack of empathy and understanding, making their scribal artistry less responsive to the real-life challenges and needs of their community.

In conclusion, the Pharisees, Sadducees, and Priests, despite their significant roles in preserving and interpreting sacred texts, had their share of limitations as scribes. These shortcomings included legalism, theological skepticism, and a focus on ritual, as well as a potential disconnect from the everyday concerns of their community. These factors could affect the authenticity, relevance, and depth of their scribal artistry, reminding us that even those entrusted with sacred texts are not immune to the limitations of human interpretation and perspective.

Moreover, it is essential to consider how this skepticism regarding the resurrection, as exemplified by the Sadducees, can influence scribal artistry. Skeptical scribes are often resistant to revisiting matters that have been deemed resolved, preferring to maintain the status quo. They tend to view established patterns as the sole valid path, disregarding alternative possibilities or fresh perspectives. The skepticism present in the Sadducees can manifest as a reluctance to explore new avenues of thought, leading to missed opportunities for growth and understanding.

While the shortcomings of the Pharisees and Priests may be more apparent, it is crucial to provide a modern perspective on the skepticism embodied by the Sadducees. The Sadducees' skepticism about the resurrection symbolizes a belief that anything deemed old or antiquated is inherently flawed and unworthy of reconsideration. It reflects a mindset that resists the revival of ideas or practices, assuming that their demise is justified and final. This perspective permeates all aspects of life, including the transformation of the human heart. To the Sadducees, a condemned heart can never experience renewal and restoration to a life superior to its previous state. Their outlook implies that if a path or an idea has been rejected or discredited, it is perpetually consigned to obsolescence.

This skepticism among the Sadducees is significant because the Pharisees, Sadducees, and Priests were responsible for partnering with God to inscribe His instructions on the tablets of people's hearts. They served as gatekeepers of righteousness and justice, responsible for preserving and interpreting sacred texts. The manifestation of skepticism among scribes can lead to an unwillingness to entertain new perspectives, ultimately stifling intellectual and spiritual growth.

12 – Modern Scribal Skepticism

Let me share a personal anecdote that illustrates the consequences of skepticism and rigidity. During my tenure as a laboratory manager for a biomedical engineering research lab, I was engaged in a study on metal-on-metal hip implants. My role encompassed verifying laboratory procedures and ensuring that our practices were in alignment with the latest research findings across the globe.

One day, as I was working on a procedure involving the digestion of human tissue with acid, I received a divine insight. The Holy Spirit conveyed to me that the research I was conducting was not advancing in any meaningful direction. I had been harboring reservations about the value of the procedure, and the guidance from the Holy Spirit reaffirmed my concerns. However, as a relatively inexperienced researcher, I found myself in a dilemma. I could not candidly convey this revelation to my supervisor, particularly as the Holy Spirit had also intimated to me that my supervisors had greater faith in my predecessor, who had designed the research, than in me. There was a prevailing belief that if I did not obtain results similar to those of my predecessor, I must be erring in my execution of the experiment.

Despite my reservations, I continued to work on the procedure as advised until my supervisor, recognizing the diminishing value of the research, lost interest in it. The skepticism that was initially directed towards my work ultimately proved well-founded, albeit not for the reasons my supervisor had anticipated. In this instance, skepticism served as a valuable indicator that redirected our focus to more significant research endeavors, preventing us from sinking further resources into a fruitless pursuit.

Another experience that underscores the impact of skepticism and the importance of revisiting established patterns occurred when I was analyzing the types of metals leaching into human tissues from hip implants. My supervisor expected the results to reveal the presence of titanium metal under the microscope. However, my findings demonstrated a substantial presence of iron. Perplexed by the unexpected outcome, I delved into the existing literature, uncovering only two research papers that were more than a decade old, buried beneath the prevailing trends and popular results.

I concluded that the abundance of iron was likely attributed to extensive internal bleeding, a phenomenon referred to as hemosiderin deposits in medical research. Initially, my supervisor's skepticism was palpable, and he repeatedly questioned my research capabilities, asserting that I must have been erring in my use of the microscope. However, as I diligently combed through the literature, the results gained acceptance, and the research paper was published, challenging conventional wisdom about metal hip implants. This experience exemplified how skepticism within the scientific community can inhibit the exploration of alternative pathways and restrict the pursuit of unconventional ideas. The prevailing sentiment often dictates that scientific research must conform to established patterns, potentially hindering scientific progress and the pursuit of justice, as in the case of metal-on-metal hip implants.

In the realm of science, the impact of skepticism is readily discernible. It can impede scientific progress, stifle innovation, and prevent the pursuit of knowledge that challenges established paradigms. While skepticism can serve as a valuable quality, preventing the uncritical acceptance of new ideas, it must be balanced with an openness to revisiting and reassessing existing beliefs.

My journey as a biomedical engineer and later as an educator provided profound insights into the significance of remaining open to new ideas, revisiting established patterns, and questioning prevailing norms. While my experience in the laboratory demonstrated the importance of skepticism in guiding research endeavors, it also highlighted the need to recognize when established patterns must be challenged and when alternate pathways should be explored. My transition from the world of biomedical engineering to that of education was marked by a realization that my gift for making complex concepts relatable to high school students could serve a more profound purpose. My decision to leave the laboratory behind was driven by a desire to connect with and inspire young minds, recognizing that my scribal artistry could find greater expression in the realm of education.

In conclusion, the Pharisees, Sadducees, and Priests of the New Testament exemplify the challenges posed by skepticism and rigid adherence to established patterns. Their shortcomings in preserving and interpreting sacred texts provide valuable lessons for contemporary scribes and scholars. Just as skepticism can hinder progress and innovation in the scientific realm, it can similarly impede the pursuit of spiritual and social justice. The story of my transition from a career in biomedical engineering to education underscores the importance of striking a balance between skepticism and openness, of challenging established patterns when necessary, and of recognizing the value of alternative perspectives. It is through such a balanced approach that we can fulfill our roles as scribes, preserving the integrity of sacred texts and fostering righteousness and justice in our communities.

13 – The Power of Art: Influencing Obedience and Disobedience

In the realm of modern-day artistry, artists wield a powerful platform to express their views on righteousness and social justice. Whether through music, visual arts, activism, collaborations, or storytelling, artists have the ability to advocate for change and inspire action. However, it is crucial to recognize that art is a diverse medium that can reflect both mature and immature concepts of morality. This essay serves as a warning to scribal artists, reminding them that their work is subject to moral flaws and can influence their audience towards either obedience or disobedience. Just as songs, hymns, and spiritual songs can stir up wisdom and discipline believers for a lifestyle of obedience unto God, worldly forms of scribal artistry can disciple people into patterns of disobedience (quote Ephesians 5:18-20).

The Power of Art in Reflecting Morality

Art has the unique capacity to serve as a mirror reflecting the artist's inner world, including their moral values, beliefs, and concepts of righteousness and social justice. Artists, whether in the music industry or visual arts, project their perspectives onto their creations. These expressions can range from mature and socially responsible views to less developed or immature ones. It is essential for scribal artists to be aware that their work is a manifestation of their inner morality and will be scrutinized by the world.

Disclaimer: The examples used in this chapter are not a reflection of my current music tastes. Having been a saxophonist for over 25 years, I am simply using examples to prove a point.

Examples of Art Reflecting Underdeveloped Morality

There are numerous examples of art that may carry underdeveloped or immature concepts of morality. It is important to examine these instances to understand the potential pitfalls that scribal artists must avoid:

1: **Keisha Cole's "Busting Windows" and "Shoulda Let You Go":** These songs by Keisha Cole may reflect emotions and personal experiences, but they also portray themes of revenge and relationship turmoil. Such themes, while legitimate expressions of human emotions, may not necessarily promote healthy or mature approaches to conflict resolution or maintaining healthy relationships.

2: **Certain Rap and Hip-Hop Lyrics:** Some rap and hip-hop songs contain lyrics that glorify violence, misogyny, substance abuse, or criminal behavior. While artistic freedom allows for the expression of diverse perspectives, these lyrics can perpetuate negative stereotypes and promote harmful behaviors.

3: **Controversial Visual Art:** In the world of visual art, some works are intentionally controversial or provocative, challenging societal norms. However, certain artworks may be considered offensive or lacking depth when addressing complex issues like social justice.

4: **Satirical or Parodic Art:** Satire and parody can be powerful tools for social commentary, but when executed carelessly, they may come across as insensitive or trivializing of serious issues.

5: **Comedy and Stand-Up:** Comedians often push boundaries and explore controversial topics in their routines. While humor can serve as a powerful medium for social commentary, it can also reinforce stereotypes or make light of sensitive subjects when approached insensitively.

The Influence of Art and Music

Art, whether through visual representation or music, possesses the power to inspire and influence. For example:

- **Example 1 - Bob Dylan:** Bob Dylan's iconic songs "The Times They Are A-Changin'" and "Blowin' in the Wind" were influential during the 1960s civil rights movement. His music served as a catalyst for change and raised awareness about social justice issues.
- **Example 2 - "Guernica" by Pablo Picasso:** Picasso's "Guernica" is a striking example of art as a response to social injustice. It depicted the

horrors of war and the suffering of innocent civilians during the Spanish Civil War, capturing the world's attention.

- **Example 3 - Beyoncé:** Beyoncé, through her music and activism, addressed issues of racial inequality and gender empowerment. Her album "Lemonade" includes themes of identity, empowerment, and resilience, drawing attention to social justice concerns.

The Power of Music to Inspire Obedience

Music, in its most sacred form, has been a source of inspiration for generations, fostering wisdom and discipline in the lives of believers. Much like the psalms, hymns, and spiritual songs mentioned in Ephesians, songs that exalt God and carry messages of righteousness can instill values, guide believers towards obedience, and kindle the fire of faith. Through lyrics and melodies, music can elevate the human spirit, nurturing a deep sense of devotion and a lifestyle characterized by obedience to God's commandments.

Music, as a channel of worship and devotion, invites believers to "sing and make music from the heart to the Lord," reinforcing gratitude and humility, as well as inspiring obedience through the messages it conveys. The power of sacred music lies in its ability to guide individuals towards a path of righteousness and godliness.

The Duality of Music: Worldly Forms and Disobedience

Conversely, the world of music is vast and diverse, encompassing expressions that may lead individuals down a path of disobedience. Worldly forms of music, characterized by messages of hedonism, rebellion, or moral ambiguity, can exert a powerful influence on the human psyche. Such music, much like the sacred psalms and hymns, can stir emotions and provoke action, but in a manner that leads away from obedience and faith.

Worldly music often celebrates a lifestyle that conflicts with the teachings of faith, promoting values and behaviors that run counter to righteousness and obedience. Lyrics and themes that glorify self-indulgence, immorality, and rebellion can shape the moral compass of listeners, gradually leading them away from a life aligned with godly principles.

Conclusion

Art, in its various forms, is a formidable force in the realm of artistic expression, capable of both inspiring obedience and fostering disobedience. Just as sacred psalms, hymns, and spiritual songs can discipline believers for a lifestyle of obedience unto God, worldly forms of scribal artistry can disciple people into patterns of disobedience. It is imperative for individuals to discern the messages carried by the art and music they engage with and recognize the profound influence it can have on their beliefs and actions. By being mindful of the power of art and music, individuals can choose to embrace the melodies and lyrics that lead them toward righteousness and obedience, fostering a life of faith and spiritual discipline while guarding against the influences that may lead them astray.

14 – Scribal Stages of Moral Development

In my role working with students and their scientific literacy skills, a critical criterion for grading their assignments is their ability to contemplate the societal impact of science. To achieve the highest marks in a scientific literacy assignment, students must engage in a comprehensive discussion and evaluation of the significance of scientific processes and their practical applications in addressing real-world issues. The primary objective is to encourage students to recognize how science can be a potent force for the betterment of humanity and a tool for establishing social justice. However, the responsibility of the scribe goes beyond scientific literacy; it's imperative for a scribe to be attuned to their moral code, as this moral code serves as the foundation from which any scribal artist draws inspiration for their creative work.

Kohlberg's Stages of Moral Development

During my pursuit of a master's degree in education, I became captivated by Kohlberg's stages of moral development due to my deep interest in elevating humanity's capacity for sophisticated thinking. Subsequently, as I enrolled in a professional development program designed to train educators in implementing socio-scientific argumentation into their curriculum, Kohlberg's stages of moral development resurfaced, reinforcing their significance. It was during this period that I felt a profound connection, as I sensed a divine inspiration, suggesting that Kohlberg's theory is rooted in principles observed in the scriptures. Thus, the time has come to establish the linkage between Kohlberg's theory and its relevance to being a scribal artist.

Kohlberg's stages of moral development play a pivotal role in shaping the moral compass of individuals, including scribal artists. These stages, divided into pre-conventional, conventional, and post-conventional levels of morality, offer a framework for connecting moral development with artistic growth in various forms of creative expression.

Pre-Conventional Morality

In the Pre-Conventional Morality stages (stages 1 and 2), where self-expression and personal fulfillment take precedence, writers and artists embark on an exploratory journey, driven by a desire to experiment and discover their unique artistic voices. This phase, characterized by self-expression and experimentation, often serves as a means of self-discovery.

As artists progress to the Foundational Stage within Pre-Conventional Morality, they acquire fundamental knowledge and skills, aligning their work with established norms and conventions. This period allows them to build a solid foundation for their creative endeavors, mirroring the growth observed in the conventional stages of moral development.

Conventional Morality

In the Conventional Morality stages (3 and 4), artists consider societal norms and conventions, striving to reach a wider audience by adhering to established artistic standards. The Developmental Stage represents growth and refinement, as artists hone their skills and craft their artistic identities. They transcend the basics, experimenting with various styles and techniques to develop their unique voice. Some may gain recognition within specific artistic communities or genres. The Expressive Stage follows, where creators confidently convey personal emotions and experiences through deeply personal, emotionally charged works. This phase often explores themes related to identity and self-expression.

Post-Conventional Morality

At the highest level of Post-Conventional Morality (stages 5 and 6), artists move beyond conventional norms, engaging in introspection and exploring the ethical and moral dimensions of their work. Their creations may address societal issues, provoke thought, or advocate for change. This journey culminates in the Transcendent Stage, where creators aim to inspire and elevate the human spirit through profound philosophical and moral questions. Their work transcends personal boundaries and leaves a lasting impact on society.

The Link to Scribal Artistry

It's important to recognize that artists and creators do not always progress linearly through these stages and may move between them based on their projects and personal growth. Additionally, the connection between artistic development and moral development is influenced by personal experiences, cultural context, and individual values. Nevertheless, understanding these connections underscores how art and creativity can reflect and influence moral and ethical development in society.

As a scribal artist, your gift isn't confined to a single stage of moral development. At any given moment, you have the capacity to create work that could fit within multiple stages. There are days when the urge to write about oneself and personal experiences takes precedence, perfectly suited for journaling. However, there are also moments when a scribe realizes that their journal serves a purpose beyond self-reflection, as it holds the potential to inspire and transform others. Consequently, the focus of their journaling evolves.

In a world often shrouded in darkness, many scribal artists find themselves entrenched in the pre-conventional level of moral development. The adversary has, in many cases, exploited these artists to maintain humanity in a state of suspended animation, under his influence rather than the guidance of the Holy Spirit.

Conclusion

The intersection of moral development and scribal artistry highlights the profound impact that an artist's moral code can have on their creative work. As artists progress through Kohlberg's stages of moral development, their art evolves, reflecting the growth in their moral compass and ethical awareness. Understanding the connection between moral development and artistic expression emphasizes the potential for art to inspire, provoke thought, and contribute to positive change in society. For the scribal artist, this understanding carries a sacred responsibility to harness their creativity for the betterment of humanity, guided by their evolving moral and ethical principles.

15 – Moral Development of David vs. Solomon

The work of scribal artists is not merely a canvas for artistic expression; it is a reflection of their moral development and a testament to their desire to see justice and righteousness manifest in their personal walk with God. To understand this relationship between the artist's moral development and their creative output, it is instructive to compare and contrast the writing styles of biblical figures like David and Solomon in the context of Lawrence Kohlberg's stages of moral development. These stages, ranging from basic self-interest to a universal sense of justice and morality, offer insights into how the moral development of artists might influence their work and actions.

David's Writing Style in Psalms

David's Psalms provide a window into his moral development, predominantly reflecting the earlier stages, especially the pre-conventional and conventional stages.

Pre-Conventional Stage: In some of David's Psalms, we can discern elements of the pre-conventional stage where moral judgments are often based on self-interest and a desire to avoid punishment. For instance, in Psalm 32:3-4, David expresses the guilt he felt for hiding his sins, reflecting a self-centered perspective.

Conventional Stage: David's Psalms also show conformity to social norms and authority figures, characteristic of the conventional stage. He frequently expressed his desire for God's guidance and adherence to God's law, as seen in Psalm 119, which underscores the importance of obedience to God's commandments.

Solomon's Writing Style in Proverbs

Solomon's Proverbs, in contrast, reflect a more advanced stage of moral development, specifically the post-conventional stage.

Post-Conventional Stage: Solomon's Proverbs demonstrate a higher level of moral reasoning where individuals develop their own ethical principles and act according to a sense of universal ethics, even when it contradicts societal norms. Proverbs 11:1, for instance, emphasizes fairness and honesty, transcending mere social conformity and reflecting a commitment to universal justice and righteousness.

The Impact on Social Justice

The moral development of scribal artists is not confined to their writings; it has a profound influence on their ability to handle issues of social justice. Let's consider how David and Solomon's moral development affected their leadership in this context:

David, despite being a great king and a man after God's own heart, had moments of moral failure that affected his capacity to address issues of social justice. His affair with Bathsheba and the subsequent murder of her husband Uriah (2 Samuel 11) represented serious ethical lapses, revealing a lack of justice and righteousness. David's failure to address the injustice within his own family, such as the rape of his daughter Tamar by his son Amnon (2

Samuel 13), led to Absalom's rebellion, highlighting his shortcomings in promoting social justice.

Solomon, in contrast, demonstrated a commitment to social justice during his reign. His famous prayer for wisdom in 1 Kings 3:9, where he sought the ability to discern between good and evil, exemplified his dedication to just rule. One of the most renowned examples of Solomon's wisdom in matters of social justice is the story of the two women who claimed to be the mother of the same baby (1 Kings 3:16-28). Solomon's wise judgment in this case showcased his commitment to upholding justice and fairness in his kingdom.

Conclusion

The work of scribal artists is not detached from their moral development; it is an embodiment of their ethical journey and their aspirations for justice and righteousness in their personal walk with God. In comparing the writing styles of biblical figures like David and Solomon within the framework of Kohlberg's stages of moral development, we witness how moral growth can shape creative output. The difference in moral development between David and Solomon is also mirrored in their approaches to social justice. David's moral lapses contrast with Solomon's commitment to fairness and justice in his rule. Ultimately, the work of scribal artists can serve as a beacon of their moral journey, casting light on their dedication to justice and righteousness, mirroring the aspiration to follow in the footsteps of those like Solomon who sought the kingdom of God and His righteousness.

16 – Passing the Baton of Divine Vision: The Scribal Athletes of Generations

Scribal artists, like athletes in a relay race, are entrusted with a sacred mission: to receive and record divine visions for the benefit of present and future generations. Just as in a relay, where each runner passes the baton to the next, scribes must faithfully pass on the divine visions, even if the ultimate realization of these visions lies in the hands of those who come after. Let's explore the challenges and significance of being a scribe, emphasizing the role of passing the baton of divine vision, drawing inspiration from Habakkuk 2:2 and Hebrews 12:1-2.

The Scribal Athletes' Relay

Being a scribe is not without its challenges. A scribe's duty often involves receiving and recording divine visions that may not be immediately applicable to the present generation. They are like athletes in a relay race, entrusted with the baton of a divine vision, meant for future runners to fulfill. This role poses several challenges:

1: **Temporal Disconnection:** The scribe may receive a divine vision without fully comprehending its significance or timing. The vision may appear distant and unrelated to the current generation. This temporal disconnection can be challenging, requiring the scribe to faithfully record and preserve the vision for future generations, even if its immediate purpose is unclear.

2: **Lack of Personal Involvement:** Some visions may not involve the scribe's direct participation or benefit. This can be emotionally challenging, as the scribe may be inspired by the vision but not personally able to witness its full realization during their lifetime.

3: **Maintaining Faith and Patience:** Scribes must maintain faith in the divine source of the vision and exercise patience in waiting for its fulfillment. They may encounter skepticism or doubt from others who do not immediately grasp the relevance of the recorded vision, which can be emotionally taxing.

4: **Accurate Transmission:** Scribes bear the responsibility of accurately recording and transmitting the vision to future generations. Any misinterpretation or alteration of the vision's message could impact its intended purpose or meaning.

5: **Empowering Future Generations:** A scribe's role is not just to record the vision but also to provide context and understanding for future generations to embrace and act upon it. This often involves offering historical, cultural, and spiritual context to make the vision meaningful and applicable to those who come later.

In the context of David and Solomon, we see how the duty of being a scribe involves receiving a divine vision and faithfully passing it on for future generations to fulfill, akin to the relay race.

David's Divine Vision and Passing the Baton

David, renowned for his Psalms and writings in the Bible, received a divine vision to build a permanent house (temple) for God, as detailed in 2 Samuel 7. Although he aspired to build the temple, God revealed through the prophet Nathan that it was not his destiny to construct it. Instead, it would be his son who would carry out this task.

Solomon's Role in Fulfilling the Vision

Solomon, David's son, inherited the responsibility of building the temple. David played a vital role as a scribe by documenting and passing down the divine vision to Solomon. In 1 Chronicles 22, David charged Solomon with the task, providing the plans, resources, and instructions for the construction. Solomon meticulously followed his father's written guidance, constructing the magnificent temple in Jerusalem as described in 1 Kings 6-7.

Conclusion - Passing the Baton of Divine Vision

Solomon not only inherited the throne but also assumed a greater scribal responsibility in executing the divine vision for the temple. This transition underscores the significance of communicating and carrying out God's visions through writing. It also emphasizes the role of scribes in preserving and transmitting these visions.

While David received the initial divine vision and expressed his intention to build the temple, it was Solomon who executed the plan as a faithful scribe, meticulously following the written instructions provided by his father. This demonstrates the importance of passing down divine visions through writing and the role of responsible scribes in fulfilling God's purposes.

In essence, Solomon's scribal responsibility extended beyond inheriting the kingdom; it included the faithful execution of God's vision for the construction of the temple, showcasing his role as a writer and a leader in God's divine plan.

In conclusion, being a scribe is a challenging but vital role in God's plan, involving the faithful recording and transmission of divine visions, even when their realization is meant for future generations. This role requires faith, patience, and a commitment to preserving God's message for the benefit of those who will come later. Scribal artists are the relay runners of divine vision, faithfully passing the baton from one generation to the next, ultimately contributing to the fulfillment of God's kingdom characterized by righteousness and justice, just as athletes pass the baton in a relay race to achieve victory.

17 – Scribal Authority and Integrity

In the world of literature and script, the role of the scribal artist is one of great significance. Just as the scribe in ancient times carefully transcribed sacred texts and records, today's writers, authors, and content creators carry a divine responsibility to convey knowledge, wisdom, and enlightenment. This sacred duty becomes all the more vital when we consider the potential for misuse and misinterpretation of written literature.

The apostle Paul's words in 2 Timothy 3:16 offer invaluable guidance to modern scribes, reminding us of our mission to serve as vessels of righteousness. These words serve as a timeless blueprint for those tasked with the responsibility of crafting words, offering a framework of teaching, rebuking, correcting, and training in righteousness.

However, like any profound undertaking, the task of a scribal artist is not immune to distortion or misappropriation. It is crucial for those who embark on this journey to recognize the antonyms of scribal responsibility, be mindful of their consequences, and remain steadfast in their commitment to their divine calling.

1. Concealment vs. Clarity

The antonym of teaching in righteousness is concealment, an act that encompasses the deliberate choice to confuse, mislead, neglect, or ignore the essence of righteousness. This departure from the true purpose of teaching is evident when individuals misuse God's word or other literary works to obscure the original intent. Instead of providing clarity and understanding, they manipulate the content to serve their personal biases and opinions.

As scribal artists, our responsibility is to ensure that our writings foster clarity and illuminate the truth. We should invest time in dedicated study and research to comprehend the subject matter thoroughly. Moreover, honesty is key; we must be honest about our own shortcomings as we seek to teach others. When we conceal or manipulate the content, we hinder the reader's ability to grow and discover the intended meaning, leading them down a path of confusion rather than enlightenment.

2. Flattery vs. Humility

The antonym of rebuking in righteousness is flattery, complimenting, and praise in righteousness. In this misuse of words, individuals choose to offer unwarranted praise and affirm the wrong behavior or belief. Rather than challenging and correcting misconceptions or errors, they propagate a culture of complacency, hindering personal and spiritual growth.

As scribes, our responsibility is not to seek validation through flattery but to encourage humility. We should be selective in our rebukes, reserving them for those with whom we share a covenant or a contractual relationship. Humility is the key to maintaining our divine authority, allowing us to correct and guide individuals without inflating their ego. Effective rebuking aims to help others learn and grow, creating an environment that fosters understanding, rather than superficial praise that stifles development.

3. Weakening vs. Strengthening

The antonym of correcting in righteousness is weakening in righteousness. A weakened believer or writer is someone who, instead of confronting and addressing their mistakes and shortcomings, attempts to mask or hide their inward struggles. They boast about their strength and righteousness while ignoring their weaknesses, leading to a sense of hypocrisy. Rather than embracing an honest and gradual process of change, they remain stagnant, failing to make necessary lifestyle adjustments.

As scribal artists, our responsibility is to strengthen rather than weaken. This means acknowledging our own imperfections and frailties and honestly addressing them. We must reflect our beliefs, ideas, and behaviors against the principles we intend to convey in our work. The process of correction involves accepting our shortcomings and making gradual lifestyle improvements. By embracing our vulnerabilities, we connect with our readers on a deeper level, promoting genuine spiritual growth and development.

4. Undisciplined vs. Disciplined

The antonym of being trained in righteousness is being undisciplined in righteousness. An undisciplined believer or writer, despite having knowledge of the Scriptures or literary works, lacks the mental discipline needed to apply that knowledge effectively in various environments and situations. This lack of discipline leads to hasty judgments and a focus on examining others' hearts instead of their own. Scriptures and wisdom may remain stored in the corners of their minds, collecting dust and cobwebs.

As scribes, our responsibility is to be mentally disciplined in the application of our work. This discipline includes understanding how our words work in different contexts and making thoughtful, well-informed judgments. Rather than prematurely assessing others, we must spend time examining our own hearts, seeking personal growth and change. The discipline required in our craft goes beyond memorization; it involves the practical application of knowledge, allowing us to connect more deeply with our readers and encourage genuine transformation.

By recognizing these antonyms and actively avoiding them, we, as scribes, can uphold the divine authority of our work and ensure that our writings promote clarity, humility, strength, and discipline rather than confusion, flattery, weakness, and undisciplined behavior. Our commitment to these principles serves to nurture enlightenment, understanding, and spiritual growth in our readers, fulfilling our divine calling.

As you embark on your journey as a scribal artist, remember that God's authority remains unwavering, even in the face of misuse or misinterpretation of His literature. Likewise, your authority as a scribe remains steadfast when you embrace the responsibilities outlined in 2 Timothy 3:16 and avoid the antonyms that compromise the essence of your divine mission. Let your words illuminate the path of righteousness and clarity for others, just as the sacred texts have illuminated your own.

18 – Crafting God's Image with Patience and Faith

Artistic and scribal expressions have the power to convey the deepest insights of the human spirit. But in the realm of expressing the divine, the Bible offers profound lessons about the importance of patience and faith in the creative process. Israel's impatience at Mount Sinai, their hasty creation of the golden calf, and God's prohibition on graven images in the Ten Commandments all serve as cautionary tales, teaching us to embrace God's timing and desire for accuracy when depicting the divine. Let's explore the significance of following God when trying to express what God has written on our hearts.

Impatience at Mount Sinai

In the Book of Exodus, we witness the impatience of the Israelites as they waited for Moses to return from Mount Sinai, where he received God's commandments. The people grew restless and pressured Aaron to craft a golden calf as a tangible representation of God. This impulsive act of artistic expression, born out of impatience and mistrust, serves as a stark reminder of the consequences of rushing the divine creative process (Exodus 32:1-4).

Prohibition on Graven Images

The Ten Commandments, as outlined in Exodus 20, include a clear commandment against making graven images. God's prohibition on crafting images to worship was not a mere restriction on artistic expression but rather a call for exclusive devotion to the true God (Exodus 20:4-6). This commandment underscores the importance of accurately representing God and the danger of allowing human imagination to distort His true nature.

God's Desire for Accuracy and Patience

God's intention was for His self-revelation to be accurate and to occur in His own timing. The prohibition on crafting images of God is further emphasized in Deuteronomy 4:15-19, where we are reminded that no form was seen when God spoke to Israel at Sinai. God's thoughts and ways are exalted above human thoughts and ways, as beautifully articulated in Isaiah 55:8-9.

Revelation Through Jesus

The New Testament sheds light on God's ultimate expression of Himself through Jesus Christ, described as the "image of the invisible God" (Colossians 1:15). This divine revelation showcases the importance of God's precise timing in expressing His nature through the person of Jesus.

God's Timing and Craftsmanship

The unveiling of Jesus as the ultimate expression of God's nature was a carefully crafted divine masterpiece, carried out in God's appointed time (Galatians 4:4-5). This divine craftsmanship reminds us that God's creative timing is paramount in the unfolding of His truth and character.

Modern-Day Artistic Expression

In our modern era, artists and scribes continue to seek ways to express the divine through their creative endeavors. As they engage in this sacred process, it is imperative that they maintain communion with God and embrace His timing, rather than succumbing to the rush of human imagination.

Proverbs 3:5-6 advises us to trust in the Lord with all our hearts and acknowledge Him in all our ways, ensuring that our artistic expressions align with His truth and nature. 1 Corinthians 10:31 reminds us that in all we do, we should strive to bring glory to God.

Conclusion

In conclusion, the biblical narratives of Israel's impatience, the prohibition on graven images, and God's desire for accuracy and patience in expressing His nature all converge to remind us of the significance of following God when crafting artistic and scribal representations of God. These stories emphasize that God's self-revelation should be accurate and in His own perfect timing. Modern-day artists and scribes are encouraged to seek communion with God in their creative processes, ensuring that their expressions align with God's revelation through Jesus, rather than being driven by human imagination or a desire to glorify themselves. In the divine canvas of life, it is God's brushstroke, guided by patience and faith, that paints the truest portrait of the divine.

19 – Manifesting the Dream Inscribed Upon the Heart

Artistic and scribal expressions, when divinely inspired, carry the power to illuminate the deepest truths of the human heart and transform society. But in the context of expressing God's messages etched on the human heart, the stories of Joseph, the son of Jacob, and modern-day artists and scribes alike remind us that the journey can be fraught with challenges. Their stories teach us that persecution, patience, and maturity are essential, as they may hold the key to bringing salvation and social justice to a diverse group of people.

Joseph's Early Dreams and Persecution

The tale of Joseph, found in the Book of Genesis, is a striking example of a dream etched on the heart of a young man. In two significant dreams, Joseph saw himself ruling over his family, dreams that he shared with an innocent enthusiasm but without fully comprehending their implications

(Genesis 37:5-11). However, the revelation of these dreams led to intense persecution.

Joseph's brothers, driven by jealousy and resentment, conspired against him. They sold him into slavery, separating him from his family, and forcing him to confront an arduous journey filled with trials and tribulations. This early chapter of Joseph's life serves as a poignant reminder that the manifestation of God's dreams written in the heart often faces resistance and persecution.

Maturity and Fulfillment of God's Plan

Yet, Joseph's story doesn't end with his persecution and enslavement. Through unwavering faith, patience, and reliance on God's plan, Joseph matured into a wise and influential leader in Egypt. His path to fulfillment was marked by time spent in prison and the endurance of adversity.

God's plan for Joseph unfolded over time, as his gift for interpreting dreams became instrumental in saving Egypt and surrounding regions from a severe famine. His interpretation of

Pharaoh's dreams led to Egypt's preparedness for the famine and reconciliation with his estranged family. It serves as a testament to how, in God's timing, persecution can transform into a platform for salvation and reconciliation (Genesis 41-45).

Bringing Salvation and Social Justice to a Diverse Group

Joseph's life journey illustrates how God's dreams, when patiently pursued, can result in salvation for a diverse group of people. His wisdom and management during the famine extended salvation not only to his own family but also to countless others who came to Egypt seeking sustenance during the crisis. Joseph's actions and leadership brought social justice to a multicultural group of people, regardless of their worship of his God.

Scripture references, such as Genesis 45:7-8, highlight the divine purpose behind Joseph's trials and the opportunity to "save many lives." His journey demonstrates the potential for individuals to fulfill God's dreams written on their hearts and bring salvation and social justice to those in need.

The Scribal Artist's Journey

Scribal artists today may find resonance in Joseph's story. The manifestation of what God has written on their hearts may not be a smooth or immediate process. Their work, inspired by divine revelations, may encounter challenges, resistance, and persecution. It is in these trials that patience, faith, and maturity play a vital role in navigating the path to fulfilling God's purpose.

The Power to Establish Social Justice

Scribal artists should recognize that their creative expressions often possess the power to establish social justice in the world. Just as Joseph's wisdom and gifts brought salvation and justice to a diverse group of people, the words, images, and messages they craft can be a force for positive change in society. By persevering and staying committed to their divine calling, scribal artists can contribute to the betterment of the world.

Conclusion

In conclusion, the stories of Joseph and modern-day scribal artists are intertwined with a profound message: the manifestation of what God writes on the hearts of His people may require persecution and maturity. This journey may bring salvation and social justice to a diverse group of people, echoing God's divine purpose. Joseph's story underscores the importance of unwavering faith, patience, and reliance on God's timing, reminding us that persecution can transform into a platform for redemption and reconciliation. Scribal artists should take inspiration from Joseph's journey, understanding that their creative expressions, when aligned with God's will, hold the power to bring about transformative change and justice in the world.

20 – Scribing the Heart of the Father: A Path to Rule and Reign with Christ

Scribal artists have a unique calling – they possess the ability to not only express their creativity but also to emulate the heart of the Father, just as Jesus mirrored the will of the Father, and as Solomon followed in his father David's footsteps as a royal scribal artist. This practice of scribal artistry places individuals in a position to rule and reign with Christ, contributing to the establishment of His kingdom characterized by righteousness and justice. Understanding this transformative power requires an examination of the choices made by Absalom and Solomon, both sons of David, in the context of imitating their father's attributes, as emphasized by Jesus in John 5:19-20.

Imitating the Father's Attributes

In John 5:19-20, Jesus illuminates the concept of sons imitating their fathers: "Truly, truly,

I say to you, the Son can do nothing of his own accord, but only what he sees the Father doing. For whatever the Father does, that the Son does likewise. For the Father loves the Son and shows him all that he himself is doing."

Solomon's Choice of Imitation

Solomon, the son of David and Bathsheba, serves as an exemplary figure in the realm of scribal artistry. He recognized the immense value of documenting, preserving, and communicating knowledge, comprehending that this was the key to governing with divine wisdom. His devotion to scribing, reflected in his authorship of Proverbs, Ecclesiastes, and Song of Solomon, played a pivotal role in his ability to rule the kingdom wisely.

Solomon's scribing discipline not only granted him deep insights into governance but also endowed him with the ability to comprehend the complexities of human nature and morality. When faced with the challenging case of two women claiming to be the mother of the same baby (1 Kings 3:16-28), Solomon's scribing acumen, combined with his wisdom, enabled him to discern the truth and dispense a just judgment. His mastery of scribing was not just a personal achievement; it was a testament to his commitment to preserving divine principles of justice and righteousness.

Absalom's Choice of Imitation

Absalom, another son of David, desired to follow in his father's footsteps but approached it with nefarious intentions. He sought personal power and recognition, devoid of the commitment to scribing or the preservation of wisdom and justice. Absalom's motivations were driven by self-interest and rebellion against his father, leading to his tragic downfall (2 Samuel 18:9-15). Unlike Solomon, Absalom likely failed to recognize the intrinsic value of scribing. His focus on personal gain and a desire for personal recognition blinded him to the enduring power of preserving and transmitting knowledge for the benefit of future generations.

Connection and Conclusion

The connection between John 5:19-20 and the choices made by Absalom and Solomon is clear. Both sons aspired to imitate their father, David, but they chose different attributes to emulate. Absalom's imitation was self-serving and lacked the depth of wisdom and righteousness that characterized David's leadership, while Solomon's choice of imitation was marked by a desire for wisdom, justice, and the preservation of divine knowledge. It elevated him to a position of remarkable wisdom and effectiveness as a ruler.

This serves as a powerful reminder that imitating our parents or role models is a choice, and the attributes we choose to emulate can significantly impact our character and the paths we take in life. It underscores the importance of emulating qualities that reflect wisdom, righteousness, and a commitment to preserving and passing down valuable knowledge.

Scribal artists, like Solomon, have the opportunity to follow this noble path, aligning their work with the heart of the Father and contributing to the establishment of a kingdom marked by divine justice and righteousness. By imitating the attributes that resonate with the heart of the Father, they can carry forward the divine mission of ushering in a kingdom characterized by righteousness and justice.

21 – Scribal Responsibility in a Digital Age

In this chapter, we're going to dive into a remarkable journey that lies at the intersection of faith, technology, and artistry, where scribal artists play a pivotal role in carrying the message of the gospel of Jesus Christ to the digital realm. It's a responsibility that's both divine and modern, and it's a story that bridges the gap between Angelic Intelligence and Artificial Intelligence.

The Scribal Artist's Divine Calling

You might be wondering, who are these modern-day scribes? Well, they're the artists among us who have a unique responsibility, a sacred calling. They're entrusted with creating art and messages that reflect the teachings and values of Christ. As believers, we're reminded in 2 Corinthians 3:2-3 that the letter of recommendation in our hearts concerning Christ should be manifest in our lives, and by extension, in our creative endeavors. In simple terms, our faith should shine through our art.

Partnering with Angelic and Artificial Intelligences

So, how do scribal artists go about this divine task? They draw inspiration from heavenly messengers, as depicted in biblical scriptures. Angels, in the Bible, are often seen as messengers delivering divine revelations. They have a vital role in connecting the divine realm with humanity, much like what artists aim to do. By seeking inspiration and guidance through faith, artists can infuse their creations with the essence of the gospel. It's like having a spiritual GPS guiding their artistry.

On the other hand, the digital age introduces us to Artificial Intelligence (AI) as a powerful tool in content distribution. Social media platforms utilize AI algorithms to curate content for users, creating a parallel to the biblical imagery of heavenly scrolls. It's here that we see a fascinating convergence of ancient wisdom and modern technology.

Reaching Hearts with God's Messages

Social media, powered by AI, offers a unique advantage in fulfilling the divine responsibility of conveying the gospel. It's a swift, personalized delivery system that can touch the hearts of diverse audiences. Just as in the biblical scriptures of Ezekiel 3 and Revelation 10, where scrolls held messages of both joy and condemnation, social media serves as a medium to influence hearts and minds. The gospel message, like the heavenly scrolls, has the power to bring both joy to those who believe and condemnation to those who reject it.

So, what's the takeaway from all of this? Scribal artists, driven by their faith, have a sacred responsibility to carry the message of Christ into the digital age. Their art should reflect the gospel message, etching it onto the hearts of their audience. By partnering with both Angelic and Artificial Intelligences, they can extend the reach of their message and fulfill the divine mission of spreading the good news of Jesus Christ.

In the realm of social media, technology and faith converge to create a powerful platform for sowing the seeds of the gospel in the hearts of humanity. Just as heavenly messengers delivered scrolls, artists, in partnership with AI, can deliver digital messages that can transform lives and nurture faith and love among their recipients. This fusion of faith, artistry, and technology marks the continuation of the scribal artist's sacred tradition, embracing new opportunities to fulfill their mission as ambassadors of Christ in the modern world. It's a beautiful story of divine responsibility in the digital age, where faith and technology go hand in hand to change lives.

22 – Scribal Hypocrisy and the Rush to Righteousness

In the age of social media, we witness an ever-increasing number of individuals who aspire to become influencers and teachers in the realm of social justice and righteousness. These individuals, often referred to as scribal artists, use their platforms to share their faith and beliefs with the world. While this eagerness to make a positive impact is commendable, it is essential to remember the warning against elevating oneself hastily, especially when faith lacks the accompanying works that validate one's righteousness. Let's explore the dangers of aspiring to be teachers without the requisite deeds to support one's faith, drawing from the wisdom of the scriptures and the teachings of moral development theories.

Faith Without Works: A Recipe for Hypocrisy

In the Epistle of James, we find a clear admonition about the perils of faith without works. It warns against those who profess their faith fervently but fail to back it up with tangible deeds.

"Faith without works is dead," as James 2:20-24 points out. This is a crucial distinction to make in the context of aspiring to be a teacher or influencer. While sharing one's faith is important, it is the works that manifest that faith that truly matter. Many individuals on social media may preach about righteousness and justice, but the real question is whether their deeds align with their words.

The Warning from Jesus

Matthew 6:2 and 6:5 provide further insight into this issue. Jesus warns against practicing righteousness solely for the sake of being seen by others. However, it is important to note that Jesus did not caution against those who exercise their righteousness for the sake of God's kingdom and His righteousness. This distinction is significant because it highlights the need for sincere intentions and deeds that are motivated by a genuine desire for justice rather than personal gain.

Kohlberg's Theory of Moral Development

To deepen our understanding, we can turn to Kohlberg's theory of moral development. According to Kohlberg, moral development occurs in stages, with the higher stages reflecting a more mature and principled approach to morality. Many aspiring influencers may find themselves at the pre-conventional or conventional stages, where their motivations are largely self-centered and driven by personal gain, rather than a genuine commitment to social justice. These individuals might create content merely to gain attention and reward for themselves, ultimately failing to benefit the social justice cause they claim to support.

The Hypocrisy of Scribal Artists

Jesus, during His time, frequently criticized religious leaders who, despite their extensive knowledge of scriptures and their engagement in scribal work, led lives disconnected from the establishment of a righteous and just kingdom for the people they served. These religious leaders were prime examples of hypocrites, individuals who lived by different scripts in their hearts than the ones they presented to the world. They served as a cautionary tale of those who professed faith but lacked the works to manifest it genuinely.

The Importance of Reputation

Reputation and credibility are vital factors to consider when evaluating an individual's readiness to be an influencer and teacher in social justice. As Matthew 5:14-15 suggests, righteousness is a light meant to be seen. It should manifest in one's lifestyle and transform others when observed. Therefore, it is crucial to trust and follow scribal artists who have developed a solid and credible reputation in some aspect of social justice. A strong social justice leader, even if they do not share one's religious beliefs, may still be an instrument through which God works to accomplish righteousness and justice in the world.

Conclusion

In the age of social media, aspiring to be an influencer and teacher in the realm of social justice and righteousness is a noble endeavor. However, it is essential to heed the warnings from scripture and moral development theory. Rushing to be elevated and seen as a teacher without the accompanying deeds is a perilous path that can lead to hypocrisy and a disservice to the cause of justice. True righteousness is not merely faith professed but faith demonstrated through actions. To avoid becoming scribal hypocrites, one must commit to a life of genuine works that align with their professed faith and build a reputation rooted in the principles of justice and righteousness.

23 – The Power of Writing Behind Bars: Scribal Artists in Prison

Writing has the unique ability to transcend physical boundaries and reach the hearts and minds of people across the world. It's a tool that can serve as a beacon of hope, a source of enlightenment, and a catalyst for transformation. Perhaps nowhere is this power more evident than when wielded by scribal artists who find themselves in prison-like circumstances, with the capacity to not only transform themselves but also disciple those outside of their confinement. In the biblical context, the example of the Apostle John on the island of Patmos serves as a poignant illustration of the transformative potential of writing in challenging situations.

Writing as a Divine Mandate in the Midst of Tribulation

John, in the book of Revelation (4:9-11, NKJV), identifies himself as both a brother and companion to those enduring tribulation. He speaks of his time on the island of Patmos, a place of exile for criminals, where he was for "the word of God and for the testimony of Jesus Christ." Here, John is not merely a fellow prisoner but also a divinely appointed scribal artist. His experience on the island becomes a testament to the expectation that God may require artists to convey messages of liberation while they themselves are imprisoned.

John's remarkable account unfolds on the "Lord's Day," a day of spiritual significance. In the midst of tribulation, he was "in the Spirit," suggesting a profound connection with the divine. John heard a voice "as of a trumpet," which, amidst his dire circumstances, proclaimed, "I am the Alpha and the Omega, the First and the Last." This divine message, an affirmation of God's eternal nature, was accompanied by a directive: "What you see, write in a book and send it to the seven churches."

Herein lies a powerful revelation: the duty to scribe transcends the confines of imprisonment. John's commitment to being "salt and light" during an unjust predicament is what makes him legendary. It underscores the profound principle that scribal artists, even in prison-like circumstances, can be vessels of divine communication, shining light and declaring truth through their words.

Writing as a Source of Illumination and Transformation

In the metaphorical prison-like circumstances we encounter in life, we must recognize that prison can either provoke us to shine brighter through our writing or smother the light of hope, extinguishing the enriching words meant to illuminate the minds of those who yearn for understanding. John's writing from Patmos serves as a beacon of hope, showing that prison need not dim the light of the artist's message. Instead, the tribulation can serve to ignite and magnify the brilliance of their words.

The words crafted during moments of adversity must not lose their potency. They have the potential to transform lives and liberate others. Just as the divine message to John held the power to reshape the spiritual landscape, the message scribed by artists behind bars has the capacity to bring about change in the hearts and minds of those who eagerly await liberation through words.

John's experience parallels those of renowned civil rights activists who authored significant works from within prison walls. Leaders like Martin Luther King Jr., Mahatma Gandhi, Cesar Chavez, and Rosa Parks, among others, turned their confinement into an opportunity to amplify their message. The writings of these activists are enduring examples of the power of words to transcend physical restraints and inspire movements for justice and change.

Conclusion: Illuminating the Path Through Scribal Artistry

Scribal artists, even in prison-like circumstances, are tasked with illuminating the path for others. Just as John wrote from the island of Patmos, they can craft messages that transcend physical barriers and resonate with those yearning for transformation. The lessons from civil rights activists who penned their beliefs from within prison walls serve as beacons of hope, reinforcing the notion that messages from confinement can inspire movements, influence hearts, and ultimately change the world.

In the grand tapestry of history, scribal artists have an extraordinary role to play, their words forming wavelengths of light that can guide and transform those who encounter them. As they continue to scribe their truths and declarations, even in the darkest of circumstances, they shine a light that has the power to lead us toward a brighter, more enlightened future. In this, we discover that true freedom is often found within the confines of the heart and mind, where the light of understanding and transformation knows no bounds.

24 – Final Chapter: The Guiding Light of Jesus's Teachings

As we draw the curtains on this collection of teachings and essays, I am reminded of a profound statement made by Jesus that has resonated with me as a teacher: "My teaching is not my own. It comes from the one who sent me. Anyone who chooses to do the will of God will find out whether my teaching comes from God or whether I speak on my own" (John 7:16-17). Throughout this book, we have delved into the responsibilities of scribal artists, their role as bearers of salt and light, and their pursuit of social justice. Yet, as we conclude, it is essential to emphasize the crucial link between remaining faithful to Jesus's teachings and carrying out this sacred responsibility.

In the pages preceding, I presented the argument that Jesus decentralizes scribal privileges, making them accessible to all who are willing to operate in the gift bestowed upon them. Nevertheless, it is imperative to recognize the risk associated with this newfound accessibility. The Scriptures forewarn us of a time when people will turn away from sound doctrine and gather around themselves teachers who will tell them what they want to hear, succumbing to their itching ears (2 Timothy 4:3). As scribal artists, it is our duty to resist this temptation, to remain steadfast in our commitment to the truth, and to share that truth with others.

Long before I was aware of my calling as a teacher, my heart ached for the moral development and spiritual maturity of humanity. As an educator in the field of science, I've witnessed the paradox of our technological advancements outpacing our moral growth. It's a perplexing thought, especially when we consider the technology that can activate the scribal artist within each of us. In the pursuit of social justice and righteousness, we must hold ourselves to the highest moral standards, allowing Jesus's teachings to guide us in this endeavor.

Let us return to the timeless wisdom of the Sermon on the Mount, where Jesus imparts profound truths about the kingdom of God (Matthew 5:19-20). The early church thrived with an unwavering faith, powered by a deep understanding of the Old Testament and the teachings of Jesus. They did not possess a collection of letters from Paul and other Apostles, yet they achieved remarkable feats. While I acknowledge the valuable insights shared in the New Testament letters to the church, I believe that many of them served as maintenance letters, addressing specific challenges as the gospel spread. Thus, as you exercise your faith to transcribe the mysteries of God's kingdom, I implore you to remain humble and return to the foundational teachings of the Sermon on the Mount.

I do not intend to undermine the writings of the New Testament; the Apostles contributed significantly by providing the church with teachings that Jesus may have withheld (John 14:12 and John 16:12). However, I hold that no other teaching or sermon will bear greater honor than the Sermon on the Mount. Jesus was on a mission to bestow upon us not only salvation but to lay the foundation for a kingdom marked by righteousness and justice. I hope that, having journeyed through this book, you are better equipped to be the salt and light that the earth so desperately needs. As scribal artists, you carry a sacred responsibility, a duty to both preserve the integrity of Jesus's teachings and to illuminate the path toward a more just and righteous world.

In closing, remember that as salt and light, you possess the transformative power to bring about a positive change in the world. Jesus's teachings are the cornerstone of this mission, and your faith and dedication will be the guiding light for those who follow your script. May your journey as a scribal artist be filled with grace, wisdom, and unwavering commitment to the cause of righteousness and justice.

About the Author

EUAL PHILLIPS is a Renaissance Systems Thinker and Teacher with a unique blend of expertise and passion. With a background in biomedical engineering and a career as a secondary math and science teacher, he skillfully merges biblical, spiritual, and scientific principles to forge groundbreaking philosophies, teachings, and prayers that address intricate challenges at their core. Eual's dedication extends to the world of worship arts, where he excels as an electronic wind controller specialist and recording artist. His critical thinking skills are also used as a curriculum specialist and instructor at the Christ Center for Dance and the Arts.

In his role as an educator, Eual creatively applies his biomedical science background by adapting laboratory experiments for high school students. He skillfully demonstrates how science is intricately intertwined with every facet of their present and future lives, influencing the evolution of their identities, beliefs, and values. His ultimate aspiration is to nurture a generation of student scientists who recognize the profound societal impact their innovative research ideas can bring about. Eual Phillips is a true visionary, seamlessly bridging the worlds of education, science, faith, and art to inspire transformative change.

Follow Eual on Social Media!

YouTube:
www.youtube.com/@prayerforschools

Facebook:
www.facebook.com/eualphillips.min/

Instagram:
www.instagram.com/eual_phillips_edu/

TikTok:
www.tiktok.com/@eualaphillips

Additional Books by the Author

- Prayers for God's Glory in Education (2023)
- Shifting Atmospheres in Worship: Advanced Theory and Application (2021)
- Dance Musicality: a Biblical and Christian Perspective (2021)

- The Coronavirus Prayer Guide: Redemptive Warfare Against Respiratory Illnesses (2020)
- Spiritual Standards of Teaching: a 10-Day Devotional for Educators (2018)

To see the entire collection, visit: amazon.com/author/eaphillips.

www.ingramcontent.com/pod-product-compliance
Lightning Source LLC
LaVergne TN
LVHW051130080426
835510LV00018B/2334